What Is a Legend?

Chapter 5
Lesson 88: Special Vowel Sounds *OI/OY*
Lexile® Measure: 590L

ISBN 978-1-62382-043-5

A legend is a story that has been told for many years. Legends are based on historical events, but they may not contain many facts or truths. Stories about King Arthur are legends. They are stories from the Middle Ages. Nobody knows if King Arthur was a real person or not. Here is a story about how the boy named Arthur became king.

The Sword in the Stone

Arthur's father was King Uther Pendragon. Many people wanted to destroy the royal family. When Arthur was a baby, his father made a choice. He would have his son raised by a loyal knight. The knight's name was Sir Ector.

Arthur was not spoiled. He had a joyful childhood. The people did not know that the king had a son. They thought there was no one to appoint as king when King Uther died.

Merlin the wizard had a plan. It was a ploy to show the people that Arthur was worthy to be royalty. He placed a sword deep in a large stone. Words were engraved on the stone. They read, "Whosoever draws forth this sword from the stone shall be the rightful king of England." Many men toiled to hoist the sword from the stone. They all went away disappointed.

One day, Arthur joined the men who were trying to remove the sword. The men pointed at Arthur. They mocked him. Then Arthur pulled the sword right out of the stone. It was as easy as removing a toy sword from moist soil. Arthur was anointed king. Merlin rejoiced. The rightful king would rule the kingdom.

Other legends tell us that King Arthur could not avoid war and other kinds of turmoil. These problems are the subject of many legends about Arthur. People will continue to enjoy the legends of King Arthur and his knights for a long time.

The End

Comprehension Questions

1. Which does NOT fit the definition of a legend?

    a. a story that is 100% true

    b. a story that may or may not be true

    c. a story has been told for years and years

2. The author included an example of a legend in this passage. What was the name of the legend?

    a. "It's a Small World"

    b. "Arthur Becomes King"

    c. "The Sword in the Stone"

3. Arthur was NOT *spoiled* as a child. This means that he probably

    a. got whatever he wanted.

    b. had mold growing on him.

    c. had chores, just like everyone else.

4. Why might people not know whether or not King Arthur was real?

    a. His name was not listed in the medieval phone book.

    b. The stories happened too long ago to find any proof.

    c. His children said that he did not exist.

5. Legends about King Arthur came from

    a. the future.

    b. a talking bird.

    c. the Middle Ages.

Skill Words

anointed	hoist	rejoiced
appoint	joined	royal
avoid	joyful	royalty
boy*	loyal	soil
choice	moist	spoiled
destroy	ploy	toiled
disappointed	point	toy
enjoy	pointed	turmoil

Most Common Words

a	he	one	try
about	here	or	trying
all	his	other	wanted
are	how	out	was
as	if	people	went
at	in	placed	were
away	is	read	when
be	it	right	who
been	kinds	show	will
boy*	know	so	words
but	knows	story	would
by	large	tell	years
could	long	that	
day	made	the	
did	many	then	
father	men	there	
for	name	they	
from	named	this	
had	no	thought	
has	not	time	
have	on	to	

Challenge Words

childhood	legend	problem	truths
continue	legends	problems	whosoever
family	nobody	son	wizard
historical	Pendragon	sword	

*both Skill Word and Most Common Word